MANLY MEN

sexy
/ˈsɛksi/
adjective

1. 1

sexually attractive or exciting.
"sexy French underwear"

synonyms:
sexually attractive, seductive, desirable, alluring, inviting, sensual, sultry, slinky, provocative, tempting, tantalizing;
nubile, voluptuous, shapely, luscious, lush;
feline;
bedroom;
flirtatious, coquettish;
*informal*hot, fanciable, beddable, come-hither, come-to-bed;
*informal*fit, peng;
*informal*foxy, cute, bootylicious;
*informal*spunky;
*vulgar slang*fuck-me
"she's so sexy"
erotic, arousing, exciting, stimulating, hot;
sexually explicit, titillating, suggestive, racy, risqué, provocative, spicy, juicy, adult, X-rated;
rude, coarse, smutty, pornographic, vulgar, crude, lewd, lubricious;
*informal*raunchy, steamy, naughty, horny, porno, blue, skin;
*informal*saucy, fruity;
*informal*gamy
"a TV show featuring sexy home videos"

1. 2
INFORMAL
very exciting or appealing.
"business magazines might not seem like the sexiest career choice"

synonyms:
exciting, stimulating, interesting, appealing, intriguing;
fashionable;
*informal*trendy
"sales promotion is fast becoming an area that product managers see as sexy"

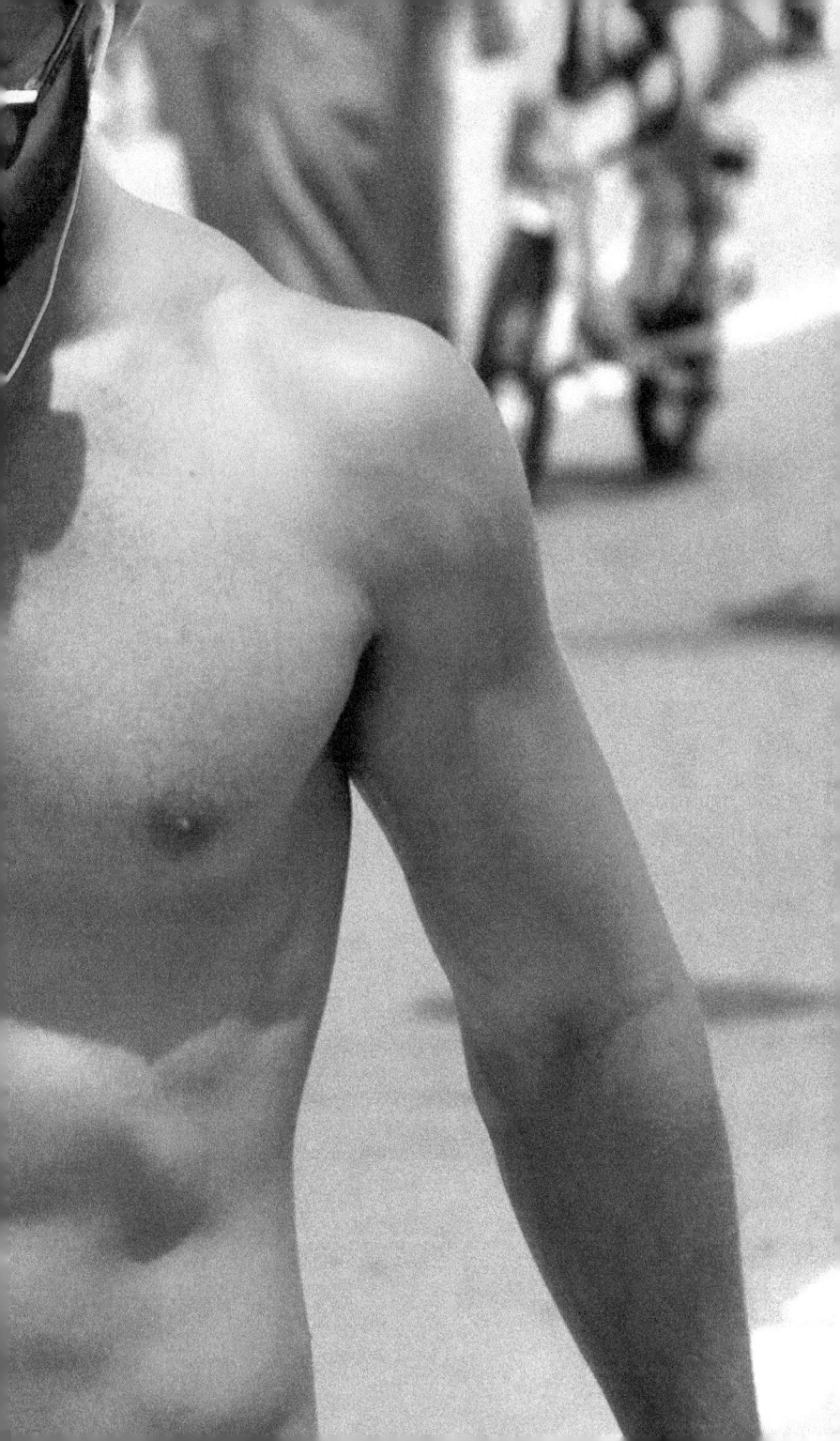

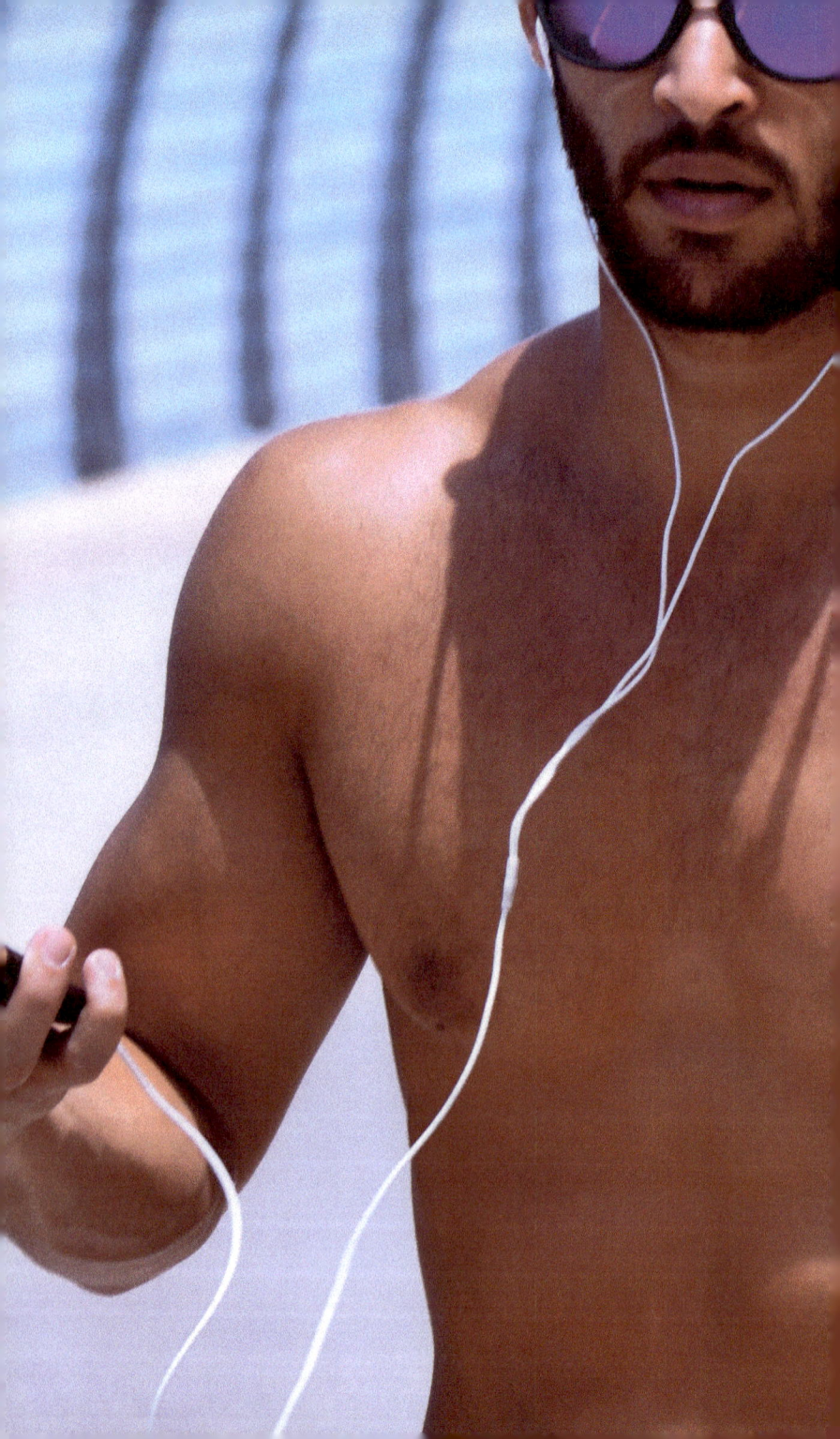

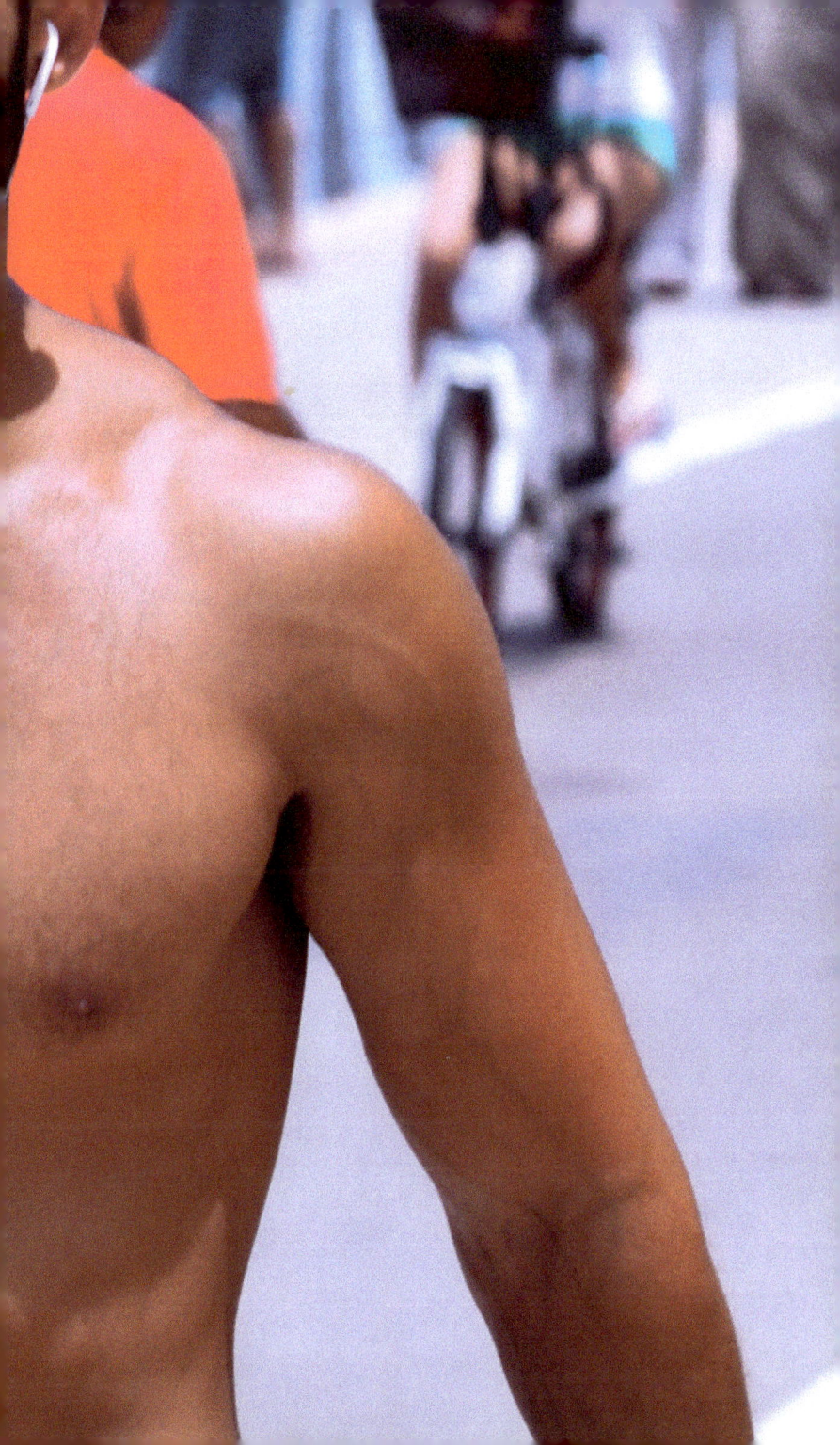

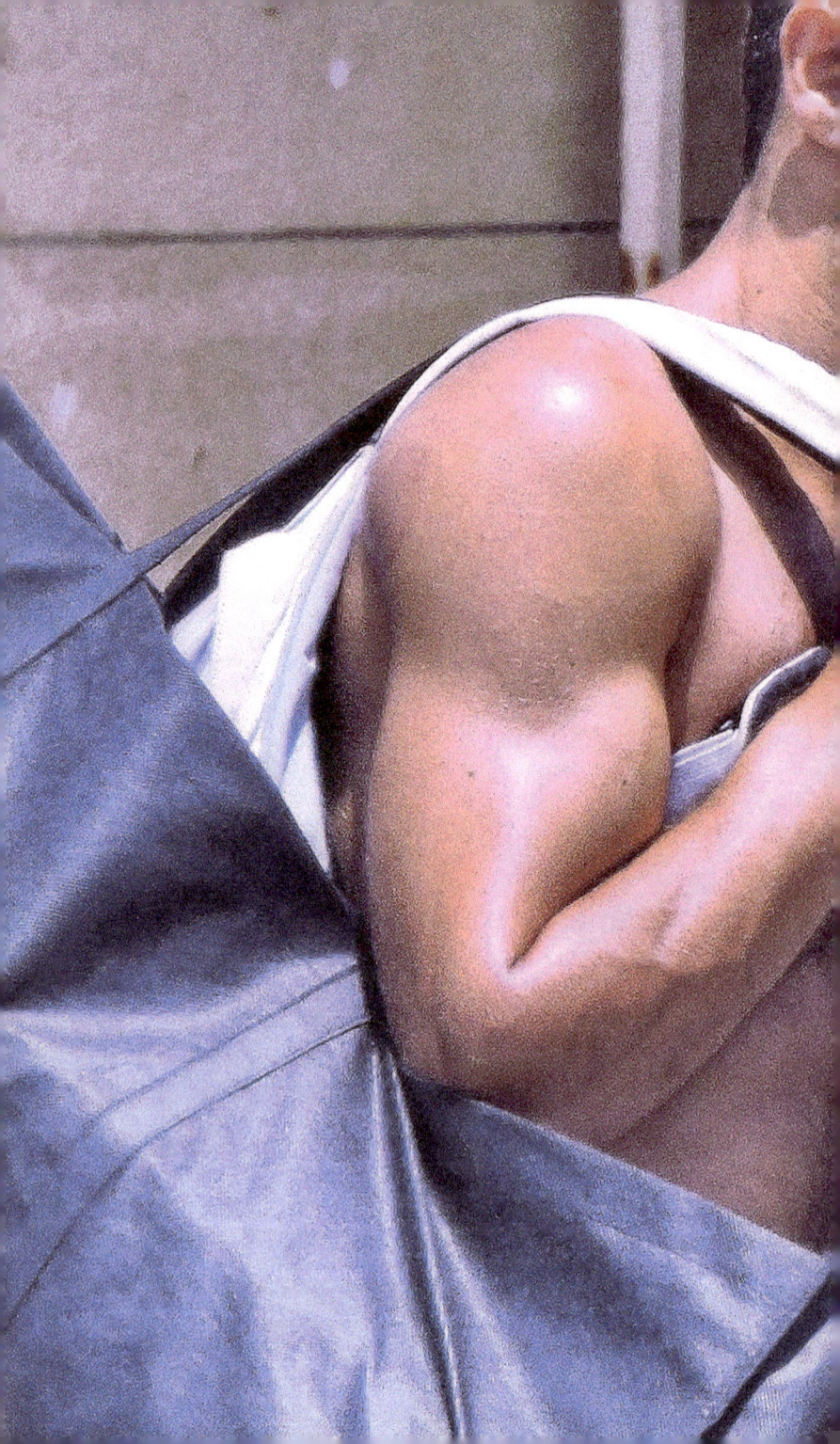

CPSIA information can be obtained
at www.ICGtesting.com
Printed in the USA
BVHW021319190619
551409BV00019B/527/P

9 780368 869105